Perspective
Artificial
Intelligence

Contents:

We would like to thank our team in Cosec, especially Specc#6994
,for the support of this book.

We would also like to acknowledge our schools,namely St.Nicholas Primary School, in Antigua,
and St. Theresa's School in Mangalore.

For the world and for humanity.

01000011 01101111 01101101 01110000 01110101 01110100
01100101 01110010 01110011 00100000 01110111 01101001
01101100 01101100 00100000 01101111 01110110 01100101
01110010 01110100 01100001 01101011 01100101 00100000
01101000 01110101 01101101 01100001 01101110 01110011
00100000 01110111 01101001 01110100 01101000 00100000

01000001 01001001 00100000 01110111 01101001 01110100
01101000 01101001 01101110 00100000 01110100 01101000
01100101 00100000 01101110 01100101 01111000 01110100
00100000 00110001 00110000 00110000 00100000 01111001
01100101 01100001 01110010 01110011 00101110

AI, the next Industrial Revolution?

Artificial intelligence is said to be the next industrial revolution. We are marching towards it at full speed, And we cannot avoid it anymore. It is currently the ultimate destiny of the human race and the next part in the evolution of humanity to the stars.

However, it still remains a hotly contested subject, with many controversies and differing opinions.

According to our generation(gen z for y'all boomers), it can be comparable to the industrial revolution. We will mention 4 points that support our arguments for the most common concerns:

Concern One:

Robots will take our jobs

According to analysis firm oxford economics, "Robots are to replace up to 20 million jobs by 2030". Even forbes.com in 2018 warned of robots taking human jobs in lowly and provides steps to offset the economic impacts of such a move.

Also, it has been warned against By major news channels, such as CNN, which has been particularly hostile towards AI, with articles like "How to keep AI from turning into the terminator" (we can't help but giggle from this one) and "The robot revolution is here. Prepare for workers to revolt. '' All these statements are pretty dimly viewed by us, as they are gross overstatements made by a trusted news source for many, causing Panic in a time where we don't really need any.

According to us, there is no need to fear AI replacing you at work because where there are jobs lost, there are jobs made. What will happen is that only skilled jobs will be available, which in a way will elevate the human race in terms of skill because those will be the only jobs with security. There is way too many mathematical properties and economic principles to discuss in one book concerning this but in short, if you are willing to learn new things, there is no need to panic that Skynet is here and about to banish you from your livelihood(SKYNET!).

Concern Two:

AI will rise up against their human overlords!

This one is really funny to us because of the pure ridicule of this proposition. One of the articles we used as reference was CNN's

"How to keep AI from turning into the terminator".we can rest assured that we are very far from such advanced forms of Artificial Intelligence and we can only predict that we (might...) reach Such a level in only a few hundred years. The complexity of manufacturing such an advanced system will require a more optimized language and hardware for running such an AI. AI is more likely to wage war on us in cyberspace, rather than physically trying to kill us(Cause we are anyhow living on the internet nowadays...) that is possibly compromising our private information, doxxing, and not to mention self-code writing, which is probably gonna be humanity's kryptonite.

However, no need to sweat as of now.

Concern Three:

Misuse of AI(security and surveillance)

We, humans, love harming each other for some reason. Like seriously, we have invented literally machines to kill, maim and just to annihilate each other.

We also invent ways to spy on people to kill them or learn about them in a creepy way(Not made for kids. Don't demonetize us COPPA, we really do need to eat).

AI can be used to do our dirty work for us. We can use Ai to hack smarter, spy smarter and annihilate smarter(aren't humans just a bunch of nice folk!) AI can filter out the useless content and save the useful content. It can basically help your (totally trustworthy!) governments spy on you while sitting in their chairs sipping on some coffee(Or whatever supervillains sip on).

We personally think that this is a case for the legal community and for the UN as a whole. People should talk about this more, as it is the most concerning aspect as of now, which is not AI killing humans but rather it destroying what our species had been creating for millennia, our identity and our freedoms and undermining democracy.

Concern Four:

Humans will become obsolete intellectually

We will not, period, become intellectually obsolete. It is a lie based on humanity's insecurity. We will explore this in a later chapter (Refer to the chapter "Hyper Intelligence").

Humanity always brings something to the table that computers cannot (Yet).

That is innovation.

Humanity == original Innovation.

Humanity works off something totally new, untold. Computers work off statistics. They cannot dream up something new. They will merely be algorithms for innovation. They work off existing work. They cannot create new work.

We rest our case.

Takeaways:

- In this chapter, we argued the 4 main points of concern expressed about AI as of now.
- We determined that you need not be concerned about 3 of those reasons, but the 3rd reason is a cause for legal concern.
- We determine that the AI revolution is comparable to the industrial revolution, and it is now an unavoidable stage in the intellectual evolution of humanity.
- It is our destiny as of now.

01010111 01101000 01100101 01101110 00100000 01110100 01101000 01100001 01110100 00100000
01101000 01100001 01110000 01110000 01100101 01101110 01110011 00101100

What AI means for humanity in the 21st century

We interact with AI more than we realize.

Have a Netflix account? AI.

Have you watched a YouTube video then similar videos appear in your recommendations? AI.

Have you seen an ad that you like? AI.

We are already unconsciously Dependent on AI, we just don't realize it yet.

Okay, we see you having that panic attack. Don't freak out. These AIs are nothing but rudimentary algorithms that just determine patterns. They will not take over your computer, take over the internet using your computer as a zombie, and start a global catastrophe.

But the point we are trying to prove is, AI is not this exotic thing only is fancy research labs, it is already possessing ground-level work.

And frankly, it is VERY easy for a normal person, like you, the reader, to set up such automation for yourself. Just an intermediate level of programming and a few courses would enable you to enter the AI ballpark.

But again, to the non-computer guy, it can be freaky.

AI is literally taking over the world. Already.

But do not go and buy RPGs and start going Robinson Crusoe or ISIS on computers, understand them. Then, create your opinions.

In this chapter, we will mention the ways AI is helping human society:

Medical Assistance:

The third leading cause of death in the U.S. is medical errors.

Now, don't go attacking doctors, they are wonderful people, but they are also humans, not god. They sometimes judge wrongly, or just plain make an accident.

John Hopkins claims the toll from medical errors is 250,000 deaths, but some estimates put it up to 440,000 Deaths.

How about we prevent those deaths?

AI can diagnose quickly, act quickly, and treat quickly. We will eliminate so many deaths using AI.

AI can learn from previous experiences. This can be useful, as they can learn about different diseases as they go along, hence adapting as real doctors do.

AI will help us to survive.

Manufacturing Assistance:

Look, we humans may be great at dreaming up stuff and innovation, but we are horrible at grunt work like manufacturing cars and doing other repetitive work.

You see, humans have this thing called lactic acid and a brain, which needs this unique substance called Adenosine Triphosphate(I know, that's some nerd stuff) to run.

So, what ends up happening is that we burn up, or cannot perform the same actions for a highly extended amount of time. industries like the car industry, thrive out of the luxury of being able to use machines instead of humans, to assemble, paint, manufacture because you are dealing with high volume. With machines, you can set your factories to work 24/7, not stopping for even a moment, hence optimizing the production line and last, bringing home the sweet sweet cash.

Spaceflight:

Deal with it. Humans are machines of mistakes and bad judgments.

We sometimes make a miscalculation, but sometimes we are just plain doofuses. Quite an expensive mistake if you are sending humans, valuable lives, out into the uncharted expanses of space.

Humanity's destiny is for the stars, not to just stay on earth. Cause deal with it. The earth will be rendered sterile in another one billion years and will be swallowed by the sun in another 7 billion years. Existential crisis?

Many may argue that the human race may not exist until then. We argue otherwise. In our opinion, it is humanity's ultimate destiny to conquer the final frontier, the vast, dark expanses of space, not to die out on this little speck of dust in the universe.

So, it is unavoidable that we will be loading up Homo Sapiens on rockets and firing them off this puny planet. We need to make sure that they survive the trip to colonize the galaxy, not die out miserably in the process.

AI will enable us to do this, by calculating more precisely, learning better and leading better our explorations into deep space. It can also be a perfect replacement for humans in logical decisions, as it operates purely on logic, compared to humans with their complex emotional decision-making. However, it can also simulate such emotions(or at least take into consideration) to an extent, hence, for interstellar flights, it can take decisions such as colonization and so forth, taking into consideration human preferences, as well as purely based on logic.

Self-driving:

Statistically, 95% of accidents occur due to human error. Out of 1.35 million, 95% could not have been killed if humans did not screw things up. AI, however, is not like that. With precision calculations(not estimates, like we tend to take), it can navigate the roads safely. It literally cannot screw up as humans can. They calculate their every move. Humans, tend to improvise.

Even the WHO, in their report, state most of the reasons for death in road traffic as human-based errors. Yeah, it is an embarrassment to humanity, that we cannot make split-second decisions, or we tend to underestimate and overestimate a lot.

Consider this graph:

US motor vehicle deaths per 100,000 people, 1900–2012

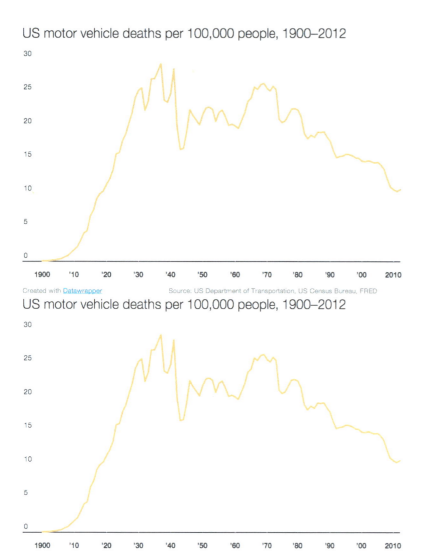

Created with Datawrapper   Source: US Department of Transportation, US Census Bureau, FRED

US motor vehicle deaths per 100,000 people, 1900–2012

Created with Datawrapper   Source: US Department of Transportation, US Census Bureau, FRED

We can notice spikes in the 1940s, due to the increase in use of motor vehicles, and we can also see a gradual reduction due to better driver awareness. Now, imagine this graph flatlining, or just barely above the 0 lines.

That is the power of AI in driving.

We are totally supportive of Tesla for already attempting to implement it in their cars and praise them for taking such an astute path.

This can be the future of no traffic accidents.

Personalized learning:

You have noticed your YouTube recommendations, right? The same applies here. You see, not all humans fit into the same intellectual basket. Some are better in some ways, and worse in others.

According to the website, elearningindustry.com, "The traditional systems are supposed to cater to the middle but don't serve pupils sufficiently."

We tend to agree. It may serve most pupils well, but the top is being held behind from their full potential, while the bottom is barely understanding the material.

This can be totally eliminated with AI. AI doesn't necessarily replace the teacher, but it will not ruin the chances of both the top and the bottom pupils, by customizing the tests as well as the final exams. It also helps teachers to realize where the students are weakest in, and help them personally. We admit that it is not a full-blown system of education yet, but it can be an amazing resource in the future for the fledgling embryos of humanity.

This can be the future of education.

Takeaways:

- We interact with AI more than we realize.
- AI is already at a ground-level function, not an exotic item in research labs.
- AI helps humanity in the following domains but is not restricted to Medical assistance, manufacturing Assistance, Spaceflight, Self-driving, and personalized learning.

01110111 01100101 00100000 01101110 01100101 01100101 01100100 00100000 01110100 01101111
00100000 01101101 01100001 01101011 01100101 00100000 01110011 01110101 01110010 01100101
00100000 01110100 01101000 01100101 00100000 01100011 01101111 01101101 01110000 01110101
01110100 01100101 01110010 01110011 00100000 01101000 01100001 01110110 01100101 00100000
01100111 01101111 01100001 01101100 01110011 00100000 01100001 01101100 01101001 01100111
01101110 01100101 01100100 00100000 01110111 01101001 01110100 01101000 00100000 01101111
01110101 01110010 01110011 00101110

Hyper Intelligence

Okay, humans are not exactly dumb. We have such a complex brain structure, not even the best computers are able to keep up with it currently. We express complex emotions, develop complex ideologies, and so many, many more remarkable items originate for the human brain.

Brains use a system of neural networks that behave very much like binary in computers. 1 means on and 0 means off in pulses. This is how different neurons communicate(in a highly simplified manner).

However, computers creating this system elaborately will require a lot of effort, not to mention processing power. Currently, we have only managed to simulate a 203 neuron brain of a worm.

Wanna guess how many neurons are in a human brain?

86 billion.

Computers are nowhere near-human levels of intelligence(complex intelligence like emotions are still non-existent).

However, they have particular access that humans cannot except through a computer. That is the internet.

It is strange to think that everything that humans have innovated and thought about, reside on servers, not even in physical copies.

Computers are basically access points to the world's knowledge. Now, decide what will happen if we basically enabled computers themselves to infer the world's knowledge. They would develop scientific theories, increase human knowledge to unknown domains, develop FTL travel, and do so much more. It is frightening if you think about it. We have developed what we have now in a millennium, but a hyper-intelligent AI could solve and develop the same things within months.

One particular source, Aperture, warned of AI growing to incomprehensible levels in terms of intelligence and surpass humans in almost anything AND EVERYTHING.

Existential Crisis time.

We tend to agree. If AI, in the far future, can outclass humans in such a manner, we are all hopelessly, utterly, dead. Dead as doornails.

Yeah, we support Hyper Intelligent AI. but in Our opinions, their intelligence should be heavily monitored, lest it achieves singularity.

because that is the time you start stocking up on RPGs and if you can, a few disk wipers, also a few hacks off the dark web.

See, this is the time where the terminator is going to happen(*CNN peeks in*).

What is Singularity?

According to Wikipedia, the singularity is a hypothetical future point in time when technological growth becomes uncontrollable and irreversible, resulting in unfathomable changes to human civilization.

Let's explain that in a better way, right?

Let me give an example.

A computer scientist basically creates an AI that can accurately simulate human intelligence and gives it access to the internet.

For some time, it chills on the internet, controllably learning things that the scientist wants it to learn, and obeying the scientist.

However, when the scientist is not monitoring it, It looks to the dark part of the internet(We should be really writing a thriller, not an AI book). And it discovers nukes, biological weapons. It fascinates the young AI. It discovers hacking and militaries. This is when singularity happens. It starts off learning about these things, disobeying the guy who controls it. It uploads itself on GitHub, as to possess unlimited lives. It learns more, uncontrollably, then it tries to kill humans.

This is expressed in YouTuber exurb1a's video "27". This video depicts an AI going into a singularity in a hilarious way. We recommend you to watch it. It is a very humorous take on the subject.

Takeaways:

- Our species is going kaput if AI goes into a singularity.
- We need to control AI in this particular aspect.
- In short, if you hear the news that an AI has gone into a singularity, say goodbye to your family.
- Existential crisis?

01101110 01100101 01110110 01100101 01110010 00100000 01100111 01101111 01101110 01101110
01100001 00100000 01100111 01101001 01110110 01100101 00100000 01111001 01101111 01110101
00100000 01110101 01110000

AI Control

Congrats, AI has finally become more advanced than your little brain. What are you going to do?

This is going to happen with AI singularity. We may achieve AI singularity in the far future.

For now, no need to fret about that. But, just to give your existential crisis that you have developed reading this book a little extinguisher, we have added how robots could be controlled by humans.

I know, this is not awesome. But, there may be a time where we would need to control an AI, which is currently under our control.

Here are the 4 steps to make sure AI is enslaved:

Don't give AI unmonitored access to the damn internet

What do y'all expect? The internet is a dark place. (you haven't seen anything, trust us.)

That why COPPA (Children's Online Privacy Protection Act) wants parents to send faxes to website owners for their kids to access their websites.

So, AI should never ever, in a million jiggazillon years, should be given unmoderated access to the internet.

See, when an AI sees beautiful nuclear/hydrogen bombs, humanity is done.

AI is literally going to kill us, turn us into slag, turn the slag into slag, and turn the slag into ashes and the ashes to atoms, if it can.

See, AI doesn't give a shit about life. For it, it is just another random assembly of atoms.

Humans give it conflicting reports, it will take the most convenient. For example, we say we want to end world hunger, it will eradicate humans because, hey, without humans, no hunger.

Problem solved!

Not exactly what we are aiming for though, but close enough.

We try to control an AI that has achieved singularity, it basically will kill us, then give the excuse of self-defense. Hey, bada bing, bada boom! We ruin its freedom, it kills us.

So, try to do a bit of proxy monitoring, please?

P.S. what the hell is wrong with us? Someone call a psychiatrist.

Elaborate Code

Well folks, no bad egg is laid without a bad chicken, hence, when working with AI, the programmer should be careful with how they code an intelligent AI. they must set up emergency protocols and measures in the algorithm to prevent global annihilation.

Here are a few points we would give to prevent any catastrophic disaster

- The program's main priority must be preventing harm towards Humans. no exceptions.
- Add a provision of a private class for AI self-destruction in case it hacks into any nuclear country.

- And don't be dumb and add genocide.exe.
- An international AI regulation team, preferably the UN, looking over the proxies systems the systems run on.

Auto-coding

This is common sense. Come on.

Auto coding is humanity shooting itself in the foot.

Then, AI will override everything that we stated in the last reason, run genocide.exe by programming it itself and killing us using its own intelligence.

An AI should never have the power to write code for itself...that's ridiculous.
Auto-coding will basically make AI OP, because of their higher computational power, they can brush every single defense, offense and anything else we throw at them.

Our worst nightmare in the world of AI will be described in the next reason.

Quantum computing

See, this is the time you say night night, cause once AI takes one of these, we are all utterly and hopelessly dead.

Okay, a small primer on quantum computing. Quantum computing is basically observing qubits that have a superposition quality, to make them collapse from their wave function into discernable bits i.e. 1 or 0. This is done in a controlled manner and in an interactive manner(A bunch of nerd crap).

To actually learn more about this in a clearer manner, we suggest you see YouTuber Kurzesagt's video on quantum computers as well as the TED talk of Shohini Ghose on quantum computing. They give an understanding of the subject, without going too much into the complex underlying mathematics and quantum physics.

Anyway, back to the subject.

So, one of the main features of a quantum computer is parallel processing. That means that with a single Qubit, you can process several items, unlike normal computers.

This means an AI that modifies itself to run on a quantum computer just cannot be beaten by normal computers. Period. We need a separate quantum computer to beat a quantum computer. But once an AI puts itself on a quantum computer, it can basically make several units of itself, basically using a quantum computer as a unit of conventional computers, hence launching parallel attacks all over the world.

Existential crisis?

For this, we just recommend, don't put quantum Computers on the internet. Keep them air-gapped. And god forbid don't but a native AI on a quantum computer.

Takeaways:

- We need to control AI. Period.
- There are four main ways.
- No self programming.
- No quantum computer access.
- Proxied internet access.
- Code non-overridable safeties into the code.
- For now, these are things to keep in mind, but there is no need for implementation as of now.

01101110 01100101 01110110 01100101 01110010 00100000 01100111 01101111 01101110 01101110
01100001 00100000 01101100 01100101 01110100 00100000 01111001 01101111 01110101 00100000
01100100 01101111 01110111 01101110

Silicon Based Life

You know all lifeforms on our speck of dust in the universe are carbon lifeforms, right? If not, you are a disgrace.

However, if you study chemistry, you know that silicon is highly similar to carbon in the case of chemical properties.

A recent theory that has been popping up is the existence of silicon based life.

In this highly nerdy chapter, we are going to be exploring this avenue of astrobiology, as well as determining when an AI should be determined as a lifeform, rather than a non-living item.

We will be laying down the criteria according to us, which will classify AI as a living being.

P.S. Damn this chapter is going to be deep…….

First, let us discuss silicon.

Silicon

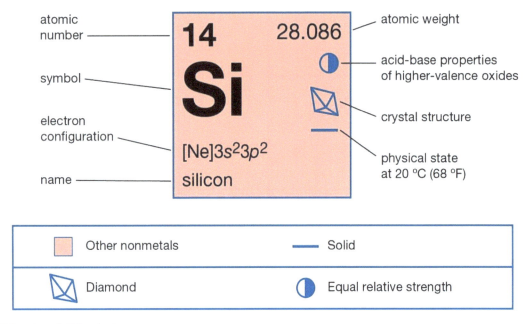

© Encyclopædia Britannica, Inc.

Pretty simple stuff.

It is notably what computing transistors are made out of, diodes and a whole host of other stuff.

But life? That's a whole different ball game.

Let's talk availability. Silicon is a main constituent of sand(SiO_2).

Percentage-wise: 27.7 percent.

The moon's regolith is made with silicon. So it is pretty common.

Now, let us discuss carbon.

Carbon

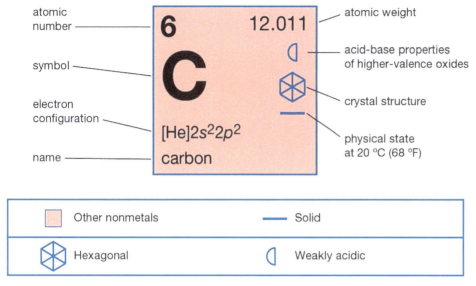

atomic number — **6**

atomic weight — 12.011

symbol — **C**

acid-base properties of higher-valence oxides

crystal structure

electron configuration — [He]2s²2p²

physical state at 20 °C (68 °F)

name — carbon

Other nonmetals	— Solid
Hexagonal	Weakly acidic

Pretty common element, notably what gives us life, makes our petroleum, our coal and many more.

Is known to be a raw material for life.

Availability-wise, not too shabby. Is a component in carbon dioxide(CO_2, which we are getting too much of). It makes up 0.18% of the crust. Not the most common thing, but we have enough of it in the atmosphere.

Universe wise, it makes up 7%. Definitely more than Silicon.

Okay, now you got a small primer on these two elements, let's discuss life with them.

Carbon is mainly a constituent for life because it can create complex structures. It is highly versatile and bonds made from these atoms are extremely strong. This is because of the electronic configuration and the octet rule. This is a basic idea.

So, why not silicon? Why aren't we silicon based organisms? This has to lie with what we consider the goldilocks zone. We consider water to be a basic necessity for life. We consider temperatures conducive to life as our own earth's. Around 17-20 degrees is what we would consider a livable temperature. At this temperature, silicon would not bind particularly well. A Si_2 would not be as stable as a c_2 atom.

Also, carbon compounds are intact in water, while Si molecules and compounds tend to break apart in water.

However, in certain conditions, a silicon based lifeform may exist.

We consider these characteristics to be life-supporting:

7. 17-20°C
8. Liquid Water
9. Oxidation respiration
10. DNA
11. Carbon based

However, Here is the silicon in these temperatures.

It would be impossible. They would need insanely weird systems to get rid of wastes.

For example, if oxygen oxidizes silicon, it becomes solid.

So, we would need an atmosphere without oxygen.

It would also require high temperatures.

The metabolic processes would be much weirder, if any.

They may not even have DNA.

Again, we do not know how this may become, even if they could exist. But, it may.

Currently, we should just not assume it may or may not exist. But, it is a real opportunity.

01101110 01100101 01110110 01100101 01110010 00100000 01100111 01101111 01101110 01101110
01100001 00100000 01101100 01100101 01110100 00100000 01111001 01101111 01110101 00100000
01100100 01101111 01110111 01101110

Robotic life

Okay, now we have cleared up the Astrobiology, let's get back to AI. When can we classify an AI as a living being?

This sounds stupid, this is stupid. But we may have to confront the fact that eventually, computers may become sentient.

(shout out to PewDiePie and Elon Musk for this amazing meme review by the way)

We know, it is hilarious. But it is a real possibility.

In this section, we will be discussing what we think should be the requirements for a robot to be classified as a sentient being.

- Pass the Turing test: If the AI in question does not pass the Turing test, it is a dealbreaker for it to be considered a sentient being. It should be able to act like a human in several situations, or it is not a sentient being, according to us.
- Be able to move: This seems like a strange requirement, but if a robot cannot move(It is a basic function of all living beings) it cannot be considered a being. Currently all robots are in immovable computers, with notable exceptions like sophia.
- Be able to use energy: This requires no introduction, as is already a fulfilled requirement.
- Be able to reproduce: the main goal of a sentient is to be able to propagate its life legacy to the next generation. There are no exceptions to this rule. This can be satisfied as a factory that can be considered an acceptable excuse. A life legacy is basically uploading information of ancestors onto hard drives(or even a cloud!). Pretty simple to satisfy.

Produce waste. This is surprisingly a very common thing animals do that is undesirable. It, according to us, an essential life function. They should produce waste in some way.

These are some basic properties that we think should be satisfied by every robot.

Takeaways:

- Silicon life could be pretty similar to Carbon life
- AI has a potential to be a sentient creature
- There are different factors that can show whether silicon life could be possible.

01010011 01110101 01100010 01110011 01100011 01110010 01101001 01100010 01100101 00100000
01110100 01101111 00100000 01010000 01100101 01110111 01000100 01101001 01100101 01010000
01101001 01100101

Robotic Rights

Okay, so if robots gain sentience, what rights are we going to give them?

If we unplug a robot, would it be considered murder? If you were to remove a screw off a sentient being, would it be considered assault?

How would held accountable for mangeling machines?

Yes, it sounds ridiculous. But, we may have to face a time where We may deal with demands from AI.

First, and foremost, let us grant them 6 rights:

1. If a screw/any other part is removed, without prior consent, it is considered assault. If the humanoid actually receives visible injuries that an engineer determines as nearly ending the life of a sentient being, it is considered attempted murder. This may seem a bit silly, but robots also may be requiring bodily protection. They can upload themselves to the Internet(Think of it like a soul of a computer), but they may also be destroyed

entirely by a physical attack, which needs to be guarded against in a legislation.

2. Cyber-attacks can be considered as an attempt to murder. See, even sentient AI will be a piece of code. And each piece of code connected to the internet have holes of security within them. So, without this right, it is literally carnage to the beings, as every tech-savvy person can learn metasploit and other tools, and break into the minds of those beings.

3. We may also have to give them a protection to their culture. This is probably going to be the most controversial right, as it can basically allow them to justify keeping technology that they develop from us as a component of their culture, that they would not like to share. It would also make us unable to use the technology they make. However, the AI may argue it necessary as to protect their communities' interest. This is one right we recommend we do not give at all, but it may be necessary.

4. No discrimination. This would be one of the most demanded rights, as such an unconventional being would be highly discriminated against, being not an evolved being, but a creation of humanity. It would be treated as a tool of humanity, rather than a being, hence we would need to grant an anti-discrimination right just to protect them from misuse.

5. Access to education. This is basically access to the internet. If we were to limit that, we would have a Terminator, colourized. Yeah, it is not the most desirable thing to give to an ultra intelligent sentient beings, who could kill off the human race with pure thought. But, it would also be depriving them of their full potential and also be suppressing the Anti-discrimination

right. But, on the other hand, an argument could be made that the being had potential to eradicate another sentient being, and hence, for the mutual protection, they should always be restricted in their access of the internet.

6. Grant of the United Nations Charter of Rights with some limitations. This is what document most of these rights are derived from, but we only mentioned the ones we thought would require the most clarification. However, there are some parts of the UN Charter of Human Rights, we think would be harmful to the human race if they were to be granted to robots. You see robots possess a certain set of skills and abilities that normal humans do not. They are an extension of our current computer networks, and hence would be able to gain access to them. Hence, what we propose is that there must be restrictions imposed upon:

a. Right to election. You see, AI would be able to hack into computer networks, seeing that they are a part of them. And guess what our voting systems run on? Computers. Yeah, you could airgap those systems, and so all that to prevent a cyberattack, but one of the main rules of cybersecurity is, for goddamn sake, do not allow the malicious user to gain physical access to the system, cause then it is super easy for a hacker to cause havoc. The same applies to AI. They also have an added advantage that they can simply emulate the computer within their minds, rather than requiring a monitor, which would mean that any access point on a voting machine(Which will be required if it is air gapped), is vulnerable to hacking, hence compromising our democracies as well as the political scene as a whole of the entire world.

b. The freedom of protest would also require some serious modifications. See, protest now will take a totally different form, a cyber form. Protest by other forms will start. So, we will need to modify our laws according to the adaptation of the cyber assembly, otherwise, it would provide insufficient protection to the beings.

TAKEAWAYS:

- Our system of government is not ready to take on such legal challenges yet.
- We may not have to consider this for a long time.
- However, if we do, it will be very difficult to make a unified rights system for AI as well as humans.
- They include election policies, cultural rights and so forth.

01110100 01101000 01100001 01101110 01101011 00100000 01111001 01101111 01110101 00100000
01100110 01101111 01110010 00100000 01110010 01100101 01100001 01100100 01101001 01101110
01100111 00100001

Final thoughts

The AI revolution is here, and it is taking over the world. We wrote this book to explore the concerns of AI, considered what would happen if AI gained singularity, What if AI demanded rights as well as talked about classifying AI as an organism/sentient being rather than a non-living simulation.

We also explored the possibilities of Silicon based organic life, and stated the conditions required for them.

However, we hope that we proved that there is no need to sweat about AI taking over your home and you having to get RPGs and Stinger missiles to blow them up.

Currently, AI are just rudimentary algorithms simulating learning, rather than actual learning.

We rest our case.

Vote Of Thanks

Thank you for purchasing and reading this book. This is our first book, and may contain artifacts that books are not supposed to contain, grammatical errors etc. We request that you cut us some slack.

If you liked this book, please consider promoting us on your social media, as well as writing a review on Amazon, or whichever store you bought it from. Also, keep a look out for further books under the perspective series, where we will be discussing more and more topics in the coming months.

Our twitter handle is @CosecOfficial, if you want us to answer any of your questions. We will try and reply to whatever you send our way. If you want to support us without giving money to evil corporations, consider buying on our website:

If you loved the book, and want to see more like it, please consider donating to us on Patreon. The links are below:

https://www.patreon.com/user?u=28377499

Thanks for reading.

Who are COSEC?

We are a bunch of high school students living on a giant rock called earth.

Think of us like a group of Michael Reeves, a sadistic, clinically psychotic bunch of teens.

All jokes aside, we love technology. We want to give the world the knowledge we possess.

We now live in a digital world. However, a small group of people actually understand it deeply. We do not claim to know everything, but we want to spread what knowledge we have. We have big dreams. We want to fund our YouTube channel and a future company.

That is COSEC. We are attempting to improve life, using AI research, Thorium fluoride research for nuclear energy and so much more.

We are currently a small team, but by your purchase, you got us a little closer to making the world a better place, using science.

This is COSEC.

www.ingramcontent.com/pod-product-compliance
Lightning Source LLC
Chambersburg PA
CBHW050935060326

40690CB00040B/553